Taking Speech Disorders to School

by John E. Bryant

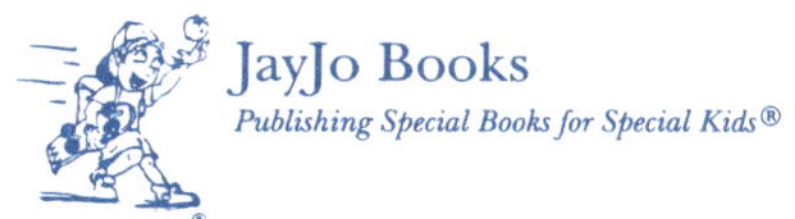

JayJo Books
Publishing Special Books for Special Kids®

Taking Speech Disorders to School
© 2004 JayJo Books
A Brand of The Guidance Group
1-800-999-6884
www.guidance-group.com

ISBN 10: 1-891383-24-8
ISBN 13: 978-1-891383-24-3
Library of Congress Control Number: 2003114683

Printed in the United States of America.

The opinions in this book are solely those of the author. Medical care is highly individualized and should never be altered without professional medical consultation.

Dedication

*This book is dedicated to all the young people
who work so hard to overcome their speech disorders
and to the therapists and teachers
who so lovingly assist them.*

J.B.

Hi! My name is Michael. I live with my mom, my dad, my grandma, and my big brother Kevin. In most ways, I'm just like all the other kids at my school. I like to be with my friends, and we always have a lot to talk about. My favorite things are skating, swimming, and superheroes.

Even though I love skating, swimming, and superheroes, it is hard for me to talk about them, because I have a problem with the way I speak.

Kids with speech problems, or speech disorders, have trouble forming sounds when they speak. There are different kinds of speech disorders. Mine is called a frontal lisp, because I put my tongue between my teeth when I say "s" and "z" sounds. When I try to say "swim," it comes out sounding like "thwim." When my class went on a trip to the zoo, I called it the "thoo."

I couldn't say the word "zoo" the way it is supposed to sound. Still, I really had fun on the trip. Seeing the tigers was the best!

Bengal
Tiger

You may know a lot of kids who sound like me, but not all kids with speech disorders lisp. Some kids have trouble with the way their voices sound. One girl I know sounds like her nose is stuffed—even when she doesn't have a cold! Some kids stutter. Stuttering means they repeat the same sound over and over when they try to say certain words.

Guess what? Lisping can be one of the easiest speech problems to correct!

In my class last year, there was a boy who stuttered. His name was Ben, and he didn't like to speak in class. He got embarrassed when he repeated sounds and couldn't get his words out. Our teacher told us to be patient with him and give him time to say his words when he is speaking. She told us not to laugh at him or make fun of him.

That's good advice for everyone!

There are lots of reasons why kids have speech disorders. Rachel, who lisps like me, has what's called a "tongue thrust." She pushes her tongue against her front teeth when she swallows, which makes her lisp. Some children with hearing problems also have speech disorders. Learning to make speech sounds the right way is hard for kids who don't hear sounds properly.

No matter what causes kids' speech disorders, you can count on one thing—they like to have fun!

Sometimes, kids with speech disorders have trouble listening too. They don't hear sounds the right way. That can make it hard for them to learn in school—especially spelling and reading. My classroom teacher, Mrs. Carr, plays a listening game with us. She gives us pictures of things from nature, like a bird or a frog. Then she plays a tape of nature sounds. We try to match the sounds with the pictures. All the kids in my class think this game is fun.

Listening better can help all kids—not just kids with speech disorders!

1 2 3 4 5 6 7 8 9
Homework
• Read Chapter 1
• Study For Quiz
• Written Reports Due
RRRIBBIT

At school, I belong to a speech club. There are five kids and one grownup, Mr. Evans, in the club. We meet twice a week. Mr. Evans is a speech-language pathologist. He helps us learn to use our lips, teeth, and tongue to make clear speech sounds.

All the kids in our club help each other. Danny and Rachel are working on "s" sounds, like me. Andy always makes a "w" sound when he wants to make an "l" sound, like saying "wight" instead of "light." Kate can't make "r" sounds the right way.

We are all working hard to learn to speak more clearly.

We play fun games in our speech club. My favorite one is like the card game "Go Fish." Instead of matching numbers, we try to match sounds. When we practiced "s" sounds at the beginning of words, Danny gave me a card with a soccer ball on it. For "r" sounds at the end of words, I gave Rachel a card with a door. I could have given her the card with the soccer ball, but I really liked that one best!

Going to speech club is one of my favorite times of the week!

r. Evans shows us the right way to pronounce sounds. We watch ourselves in a mirror while we imitate the way he says them.

To make a good "s" sound, I keep my teeth closed and point the tip of my tongue towards the roof of my mouth. Then I make air flow in my mouth. Try it for yourself!

If I put my tongue in the right place, I can say skate and swim and superhero without any trouble!

All the kids in the club practice saying sounds the right way. We even practice saying them the wrong way to learn the difference in how they sound and feel. When we can say our sounds the right way, we use them in words. Then we use the words in sentences. Finally we put the sentences together and have a whole conversation. That's the most fun of all!

Speech club is like playing with blocks. Instead of starting with one block and making a whole building, I start with my "s" sound and I keep working until I can have a whole conversation.

You may be surprised that some grownups had speech disorders when they were kids. You sure can't tell when you listen to them now! I bet those grownups had speech teachers just like Mr. Evans. Every day, I'm going to practice what Mr. Evans teaches me.

And then I'm going to have fun skating and swimming… and dreaming up new superheroes!

1. **What is a speech disorder?**
    A speech disorder is a condition that makes it hard to form sounds the right way. There are many different kinds of speech disorders; lisping and stuttering are two speech disorders that a lot of kids have.

2. **Why do kids have speech disorders?**
    There are different reasons. A lot of kids with speech disorders can't use their lips, tongue, and teeth the right way when they form sounds. Some kids have speech disorders because they have a hearing impairment.

3. **Can a kid with a speech disorder be smart?**
    Yes, having a speech disorder has nothing to do with being smart.

4. **Why do some kids with speech disorders have trouble reading and writing?**
    Some kids with speech disorders also have trouble listening, so they don't hear sounds the right way. That can make it harder for them to learn to read and write. They may need a little extra help.

5. **What should you do if you don't understand me?**
    Give me time to say my words. If you still don't understand, we can ask a grownup to help us.

6. **What are some ways kids with speech disorders can get
    help in school?**
    They can go to speech therapy. Their classroom teacher can also do
    activities that will help them learn to listen better.

7. **What do speech-language pathologists do?**
    Speech-language pathologists help kids learn to speak more clearly. They
    figure out what kind of speech problem a kid has. Then they plan the
    best way to help that child. They can help grownups too!

8. **How can you help a friend with a speech disorder?**
    Listen carefully and patiently to what your friend
    is saying.

9. **What do kids do in a speech therapy group?**
    They learn to make sounds the right way. They
    may also learn to use a clearer voice, to speak
    more smoothly, and to understand better.
    And they practice—a lot!

10. **Will kids who have speech disorders have them as grownups?**
    Speech therapy helps kids learn to speak correctly. Some grownups you
    know may have had speech disorders when they were children, and I bet
    you can't even tell!

TEN TIPS FOR TEACHERS

 **1. LEARN ABOUT YOUR STUDENT.**
Children with speech disorders are unique individuals. Learn what activities your student particularly likes, and encourage him to participate in them. His speech-language pathologist can suggest which of these activities are most helpful. The child's former teachers may also be able to provide helpful tips, and at the end of the school year, you can share what you've learned about the child with his next teacher.

2. RECOGNIZE THE NEED FOR EARLY EVALUATION OF SPEECH DISORDERS.
If you think a child may have a speech disorder, it is important for her to be evaluated by a speech-language pathologist. Children develop speaking skills at different rates and in different ways. A speech-language pathologist will be able to tell you if what you are hearing is part of normal development, or if, in fact, the child needs therapy. Early detection and treatment are essential to help the student learn to speak correctly.

 **3. BE A SUPPORT FOR YOUR STUDENT.**
Try to build a relationship in which the child is comfortable sharing his feelings with you, and be particularly aware of indications that he is feeling sad or excluded. Simply maintaining eye contact with a child who is struggling to speak can help. If it seems appropriate, refer your student to the school nurse, social worker, etc.

4. ENCOURAGE AN INCLUSIVE ATTITUDE IN THE CLASSROOM.
While children have individual differences, they are alike in many ways. Although your student has a speech disorder, she undoubtedly shares interests, concerns, and ideas with many other children in the class. Encourage the group to focus on ways they are alike, and help to develop tolerance of differences.

 **5. BE SENSITIVE TO A STUDENT'S CONCERN ABOUT READING OUT LOUD.**
Children with speech disorders may be uncomfortable reading out loud. One solution is to talk with the child about how to handle this concern. For example, you might agree not to call on the child unless she volunteers.

 **6. SET FIRM LIMITS TO AVOID TEASING.**
You can help to protect a child with a speech disorder from imitation or mocking by having firm classroom limits that don't allow for these behaviors.

 **7. ALLOW MODIFICATIONS.**
To help the student who lives with a speech disorder, request materials and equipment, such as a tape recorder or an auditory trainer.

 **8. USE A TEAM APPROACH.**
View the adults who work with the student—parents/caregivers, teachers, psychologists, and speech-language pathologists—as a team. Encourage a united approach in helping the child who has a speech disorder.

 **9. LEARN ABOUT SPEECH DISORDERS.**
There are thousands of children living with speech disorders. The American Speech-Language-Hearing Association and your local association are great sources of helpful information.

10. EDUCATE YOUR STUDENTS ABOUT SPEECH DISORDERS.
Children who are informed about speech disorders are more likely to act responsibly. If your student agrees, invite his speech-language pathologist to talk to the class about speech disorders. Have the class do research to learn more about speech disorders.

ADDITIONAL RESOURCES

**American Speech-Language-
Hearing Association**
10801 Rockville Pike
Rockville, MD 20852
1-800-638-8255
www.asha.org/about/contacts.cfm

**Childhood Apraxia of Speech Association
of North America (CASANA)**
123 Eisele Road
Cheswick, PA 15024
412-343-7102
www.apraxia-kids.org

The Council for Exceptional Children
1110 North Glebe Road, Suite 300
Arlington, VA 22201-5704
1-888-CEC-SPED
www.cec.sped.org/

**National Dissemination Center
for Children with Disabilities**
P.O. Box 1492
Washington, DC 20013
(800) 695-0285
www.nichcy.org

**National Institute on Deafness and Other
Communication Disorders**
National Institutes of Health
31 Center Drive, MSC 2320
Bethesda, MD 20892-2320
1-800-241-1044
www.nidcd.nih.gov/about/learn/index.asp

National Stuttering Association (NSA)
4071 East La Palma Avenue, Suite A
Anaheim Hills, CA 92807
1-800-364-1677
www.nsastutter.org

The *Special Kids in School*® series is designed to be read in the classroom in order to normalize and provide understanding of conditions. The books are designed to show the chronically ill child's peers that he/she is just like them but with special challenges that he/she faces with courage and fortitude everyday. When children understand conditions such as childhood diabetes, asthma, autism, allergies, A.D.D., and other illnesses, they lose their fear, better understand their classmate, and embrace him/her as a friend.

The *Special Kids in School*® series titles include:

Taking A.D.D. to School
Taking Arthritis to School
Taking Asthma to School
Taking Autism to School
Taking Cancer to School
Taking Cerebral Palsy to School
Taking Cystic Fibrosis to School
Taking Depression to School
Taking Diabetes to School
Taking Down Syndrome to School
Taking Dyslexia to School
Taking Food Allergies to School
Taking Hearing Impairment to School
Taking Seizure Disorders to School
Taking Speech Disorders to School
Taking Tourette Syndrome to School
Taking Visual Impairment to School
Taking Weight Problems to School

To order additional copies of this book or inquire about our quantity discounts for schools, hospitals, and affiliated organizations, contact us at 1-800-999-6884.